ALTERNATOR
BOOKS™

Cosmos Chronicles
Revolutionary Robots in Space

Rachael L. Thomas

Lerner Publications ◆ Minneapolis

Lerner Publications Company
A division of Lerner Publishing Group, Inc.
241 First Avenue North
Minneapolis, MN 55401 USA

For reading levels and more information, look up this title at www.lernerbooks.com.

Main body text set in Caecilia LT Std 11.25/20
Typeface provided by Adobe Systems.

Photo Acknowledgements
The images in this book are used with permission of: © NASA on The Commons/Flickr, pp. 4-5; © NASA/ESA-D. Ducros, p. 5 (left); © NASA/JPL-Caltech, pp. 5 (middle), 7 (bottom), 8, 16–17, 20, 21, 23 (bottom); © NASA/JPL-Caltech/Wikimedia Commons, pp. 5 (right), 24; © NASA/NSSDC/Wikimedia Commons, p. 6; © NASA, pp. 7 (top, middle left), 11, 12, 25 (bottom), 27 (bottom); © NSSDC, NASA/Rotem Dan/Wikimedia Commons, p. 7 (middle right); © NASA/JPL-Caltech/Cornell/Arizona State Univ., p. 9 (top); © NASA/JPL/Wikimedia Commons, p. 9 (bottom); © NASA Johnson/Flickr, p. 10; © NASA/Wikimedia Commons, pp. 13, 19; © NASA/Emmett Given, p. 14; ©NASA/Bill Stafford, p. 15; ©NASA/JPL-Caltech/Stanford, p. 17; © ESA/DLR/T. Bourry/Airbus, p. 18; © Stone Aerospace, p. 22; © Stone Aerospace, photographer Evan Clark, p. 23 (top); © NASA/JPL-Caltech/MSSS/JHU-APL, p. 25 (top); © Ievgeniia Lytvynovych/iStockphoto, p. 26 (cicada); © NASA/JPL/University of Arizona, p. 26 (background); © NASA/JPL, p. 27 (top); © NASA-GSFC/SVS, NASA/JPL-Caltech/Southwest Research Institute, p. 28; © Deutschen Zentrum für Luft- und Raumfahrt/Wikimedia Commons, p. 29 (top); © Gary Gershoff/Getty Images, p. 29 (bottom).

Cover: © NASA
Design elements: © NASA/JPL-Caltech/STScI/IRAM

Library of Congress Cataloging-in-Publication Data

The Cataloging-in-Publication Data for *Revolutionary Robots in Space* is on file at the Library of Congress.
ISBN 978-1-5415-5594-5 (lib. bdg.)
ISBN 978-1-5415-7370-3 (pbk.)
ISBN 978-1-5415-5642-3 (eb pdf)

Manufactured in the United States of America
1 – CG – 7/15/19

Contents

Space Pioneers

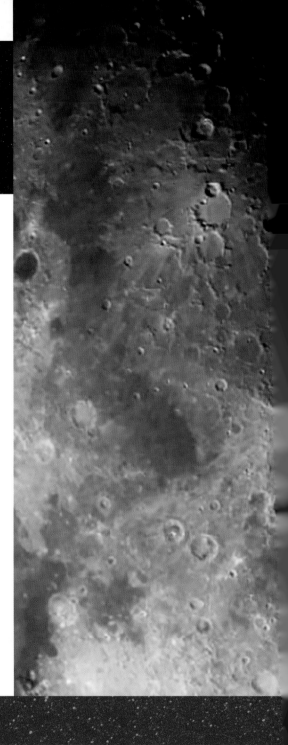

More than fifty years ago, Neil Armstrong took his first steps on the moon. But humankind was just catching up to the moon's first visitors: robots!

Robots beat humans to the surface of the moon by ten years. Scientists use robots to gather information and explore space conditions that would kill humans. This includes **extreme** temperatures and cosmic radiation.

As **technology** advances on Earth, space robots are set to become faster, smarter, and more **efficient**. The future of human space exploration depends on the robots we will send to lead the way!

BOTS BLASTING THROUGH SPACE

Robots have visited Venus, Mars, Titan, and Jupiter. Some have touched down on comets and asteroids. Others have entered the unknown depths of space.

An illustration of a NASA robotic explorer orbiting the moon

Robots Reach Space!

The first robot to reach space was launched in October 1957 by the Soviet Union. Sputnik zipped around Earth every ninety-eight minutes for twenty-one days. The **satellite** fascinated the public. People huddled in their yards after dark, searching for a flash of the cosmic robot.

But Sputnik's success also made some people upset. The United States and Soviet Union were in a race to reach space. US officials were shocked the Soviet Union had pulled ahead. US citizens were too. One year after Sputnik's launch, the US founded the National Aeronautics and Space Administration (NASA).

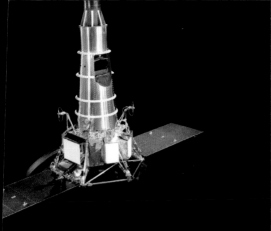

MOON BOTS

In the 1960s, NASA launched groups of robots to the moon to gather information.

Ranger robots *(left)* took close-up photos of the moon's surface.

Surveyor robots *(bottom left)* took samples of lunar soil.

Lunar Orbiter robots *(below)* took photos of the moon from its **orbit**.

DEEP-SPACE PROBE ROBOTS

In 1977, NASA launched twin **probes** Voyager 1 and Voyager 2. In 2012, these robotic spacecraft became the first human-made objects to travel beyond our solar system!

Did a Mars Robot Find Alien Evidence?

NASA's Curiosity rover landed on Mars in 2012. In 2013, it was the first robot to **analyze** a Martian rock sample. Scientists found important chemicals for life in this sample, including oxygen, hydrogen, and carbon. This means Mars could have supported life at some point in the past!

Curiosity has many tools to gather information about Mars. This includes cameras and a giant robotic arm. The robot also has a laser that can vaporize Martian rock from 30 feet (9 m) away!

STRANGE SPACE DUST

Martian dust is very fine-grained, and it sticks to objects with static electricity. This dust has led to the failure of Martian rovers. It covered some bots' solar panels, causing their batteries to die.

MARTIAN BOTS

The first robot on Mars was the Sojourner rover *(bottom right)* in 1997. It lasted three months before failure. In 2004, NASA landed rovers Spirit *(left)* and Opportunity *(top right)* on Mars. Spirit lasted seven years. Opportunity was still sending out beeps in 2018!

Legless, Humanlike Robot Roams the ISS

Robonaut 2 is a robot NASA built to look like a human. At first, it was just a head, arms, and torso. In 2011, NASA launched Robonaut 2 to the International Space Station (ISS), where it would aid astronauts with tasks.

In 2014, NASA decided to give Robonaut 2 legs to help it move around more easily. NASA sent long, wiggly robot legs to the ISS. But when ISS astronauts attached the legs, Robonaut 2 malfunctioned.

Robonaut 2 sat aboard the ISS mostly broken for the next four years. In 2018, the bot was sent back to Earth for repairs. NASA hopes to send Robonaut 2 on another space mission. Whether the bot will have legs or not is unknown!

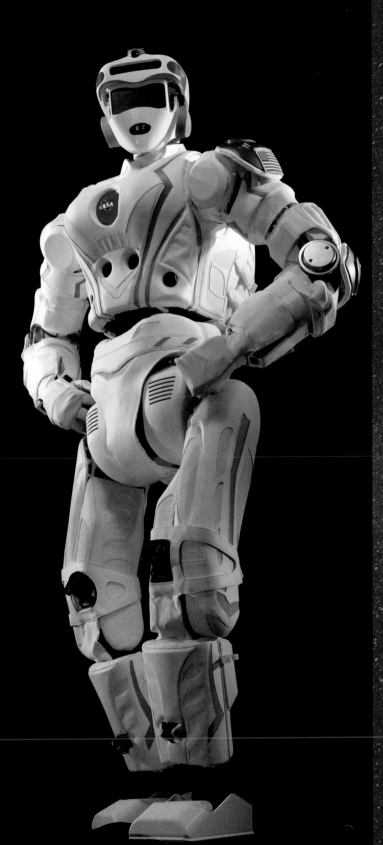

RISK-TAKING ROBOTS

In 2013, NASA began developing humanoid robot R5. In the following years, scientists began redesigning the bot for space travel. They hope future versions of R5 will be able to perform **spacewalks** and other risky space tasks in place of humans.

Space Station Sports Walking Arm

Just like human arms, robotic arms can hold, grab, or move objects. But some robotic arms, like Canadarm2, can do much more!

Canadarm2 is a 56-foot (17 m) long robotic arm attached to the ISS. But Canadarm2 is not **permanently** attached by one end like a typical arm. Instead, it "walks" around the outside of the station by **alternating** which end is attached at a time.

Robotic arms often serve as important tools when problems arise in space, such as electrical failures. They also help astronauts complete tasks on risky spacewalks.

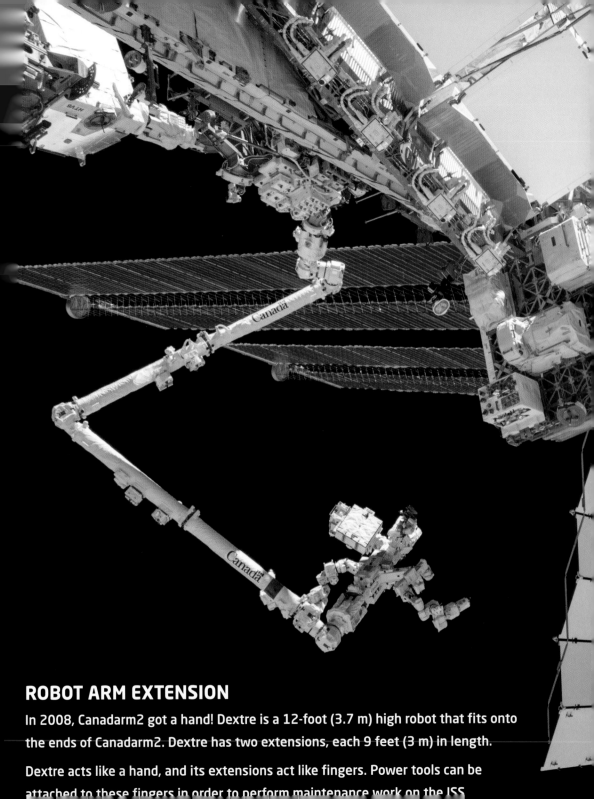

ROBOT ARM EXTENSION

In 2008, Canadarm2 got a hand! Dextre is a 12-foot (3.7 m) high robot that fits onto the ends of Canadarm2. Dextre has two extensions, each 9 feet (3 m) in length.

Dextre acts like a hand, and its extensions act like fingers. Power tools can be attached to these fingers in order to perform maintenance work on the ISS.

The ISS Made in Space 3-D printer

Galactic Printers

Scientists dream of sending humans to live on Mars. But this will be tricky to accomplish. It takes at least nine months to travel to Mars. Humans on Mars wouldn't be able to wait this long for tools and supplies to arrive from Earth.

Enter the 3-D space printer! 3-D printers could allow future Martian colonies to build what they need exactly when they need it.

In 2016, the first zero-gravity 3-D printer was permanently installed on the ISS. It was produced by US company Made in Space.

Soon after installation, an ISS astronaut needed a special **wrench** to complete a task. Within five days, Made in Space designed the wrench on Earth, sent instructions to the printer, and the astronaut had the tool in hand!

EXTRATERRESTRIAL OPINION
"It was so tense leading up to that first time the printer turned on. . . . And then comes the moment to finally turn it on and operate it, and it works. That moment marked the first time in the history of humanity that mankind had manufactured anything off the face of planet Earth."
—Jason Dunn, co-founder of Made in Space

Origami Robot Accomplice

Sometimes giant space robots aren't the right size for a task or mission. As a solution, NASA scientists are creating small companion bots! PUFFER is one.

PUFFER stands for Pop-Up Flat Folding Explorer Robot. The lightweight robot was inspired by the paper-folding art origami. PUFFER can flatten itself in order to squeeze under ledges, drop into craters, skitter up steep slopes, and more.

PUFFER was made to help larger robots navigate tight or tricky landforms on Mars. Scientists hope the small bot may one day accompany rovers on a space mission to the planet.

SPIKY HEDGEHOG SPACE ROBOT

Another tiny space bot NASA is developing is Hedgehog. The robot is spiky, cube shaped, and designed to operate on any of its six sides. This allows it to explore space environments with no risk of being **stranded** upside down! NASA hopes to send Hedgehog to explore asteroids or comets.

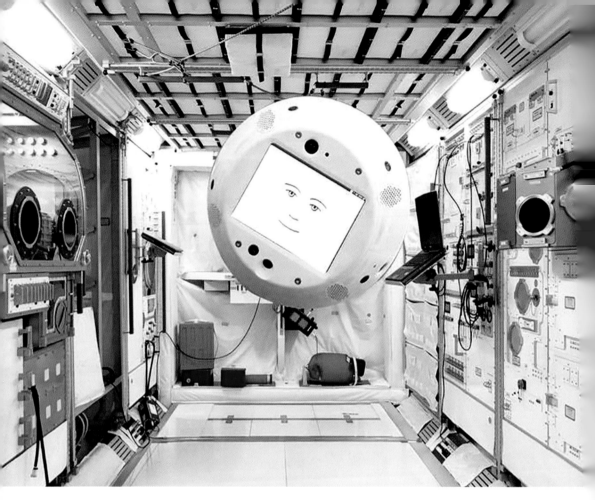

Flying Brain Aboard the ISS!

In June 2018, something the European Space Agency (ESA) calls a "flying brain" was sent to the ISS. This brain-like object is actually an 11-pound (5 kg) robot the agency developed. The bot is called CIMON, which stands for Crew Interactive Mobile Companion.

CIMON is **unique** among robots that have visited the ISS because it uses artificial intelligence (AI). This means the flying brain can learn as it goes. It can make reasoned judgements and decisions, similar to a *real* brain! CIMON can also talk to astronauts and even tell individuals apart using facial recognition software.

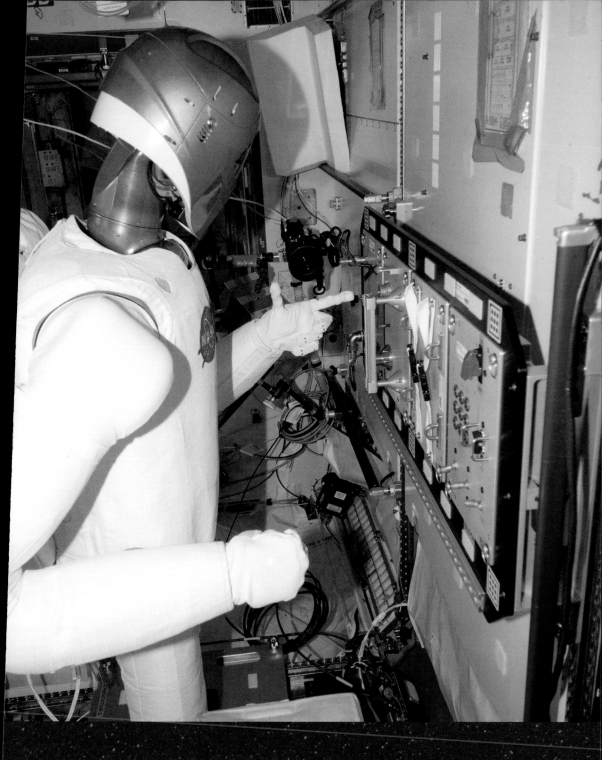

ARTIFICIAL INTELLIGENCE IN SPACE

AI allows robots to solve problems as they arise. This includes repairing themselves when they malfunction! This becomes more valuable the farther a robot travels from Earth.

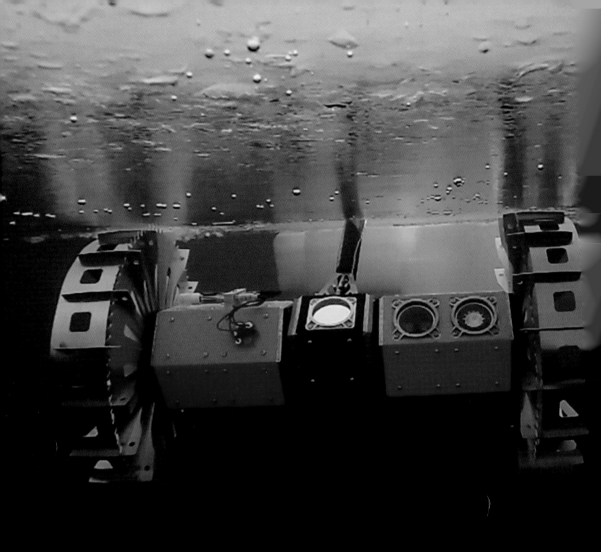

Ice-Skating Space Bot

BRUIE is a space robot NASA is creating for a special type of space mission. BRUIE stands for Buoyant Rover for Under-Ice Exploration. The robot is designed to explore icy climates, such as Jupiter's moon Europa.

BRUIE can float, but not swim, in water. It also has wheels to crawl along the underside of ice sheets! BRUIE takes photographs and collects data, even while traveling through these extreme environments.

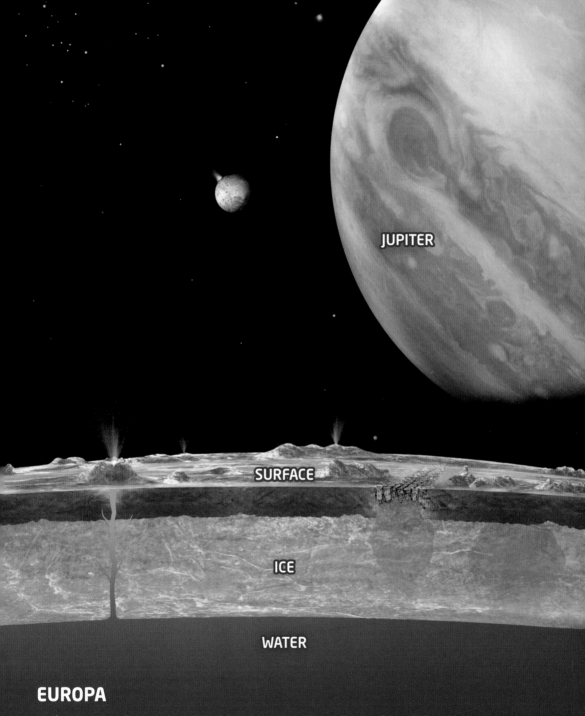

JUPITER

SURFACE

ICE

WATER

EUROPA

Jupiter's moon Europa has a solid core and an outer layer of ice. Scientists have discovered that there is also a large body of water underneath the ice.

Water is essential to life on Earth. So, where there is water, some scientists guess there may be life. Many believe there might be life in Europa's oceans!

Space Submarine to Swim Icy Cosmic Oceans

Here on Earth, **submarines** explore the ocean's depths. Now, one will explore oceans in space! Using a grant from NASA, Stone Aerospace has developed a submarine bot called ARTEMIS.

Researchers plan for ARTEMIS to swim through hidden oceans on Jupiter's moon Europa. The company tested the robot in freezing Antarctic waters.

But to explore the chilly waters on Europa, the bot will first have to break through the planet's icy surface. The moon's oceans are covered by a layer of ice between 10 and 15 miles (16 and 24 km) thick!

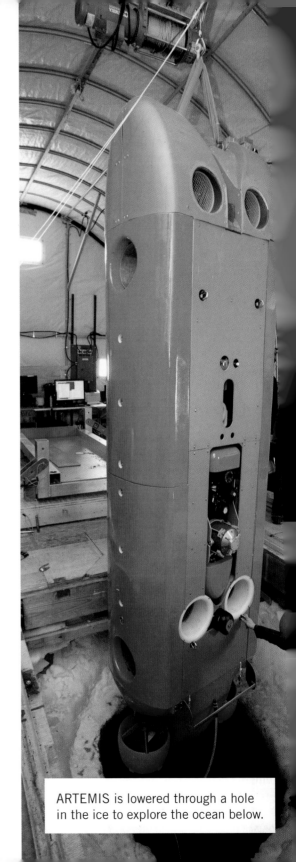

ARTEMIS is lowered through a hole in the ice to explore the ocean below.

Part of the NASA-funded VALKYRIE project, developed at Stone Aerospace. This project created a bot that could melt through ice.

BREAKING THE ICE

Stone Aerospace engineers are figuring out a way to get a robot to break through Europa's thick ice layer to allow exploration of its oceans. One idea is using a nuclear-powered laser to cut through the ice!

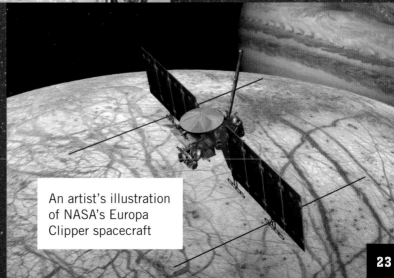

SCOPING OUT SPACE MOONS

NASA's mission Europa Clipper will send a spacecraft to orbit Jupiter in the 2020s. The spacecraft will also gather information about Europa.

An artist's illustration of NASA's Europa Clipper spacecraft

An artist's illustration of the Mars 2020 rover

Mission: Martian Life

In 2020, NASA will send a special bot to Mars called Mars 2020. The robot's mission will focus solely on past and future life on the planet. The rover will search directly for **evidence** of past life on Mars.

The rover will also undertake tests to determine whether humans could live on Mars. One test is to create breathable oxygen from the Martian atmosphere. If this test succeeds, a future human colony might be able to produce the oxygen needed for long-term survival on the planet!

NASA has chosen Mars' Jezero Crater delta as the Mars 2020 landing site.

BACKSTORY: MARS APPROACH

Earth and Mars both have egg-shaped orbits. The two planets are constantly moving toward each other and then away again. The point when Mars is closest to Earth is called the Mars Approach. This happens about every twenty-six months. The Mars 2020 mission lines up with the next Mars Approach!

A cicada flies over Mars in an imagined scene inspired by future Marsbees missions.

Robot Insects to Swarm Space

Imagine a cloud of robotic insects swarming space! A team of Japanese and American engineers are working to create this scene. These scientists are making robot drones inspired by bugs. The micro-bots are the size of bumblebees and called "Marsbees." Their wing design is based on that of a **cicada**.

Rover wheels often struggle over Mars' uneven and rocky surface. Scientists hope a swarm of Marsbees would zoom farther and faster across the Martian surface. These tiny bots would work as a team to collect data.

A 3-D map of mountains on Earth, created by NASA technology. Marsbees will create similar maps of Mars.

BUG BOTS TO FILM MARS

Each Marsbee would carry a little video camera to construct 3-D maps of the environment. The rovers would act as Marsbees central command centers where the bots would download information and charge their batteries.

EXTRATERRESTRIAL OPINION

"I'm very strongly in favor of doing as much robotic exploration of Mars as we can possibly do before we actually send people to Mars, in large part because I'm concerned about contaminating Mars, just in case there's any life there already."

—Dr. David Weintraub, Vanderbilt University astronomer

Cosmos Exclusive!

What's new and upcoming in space robot technology?

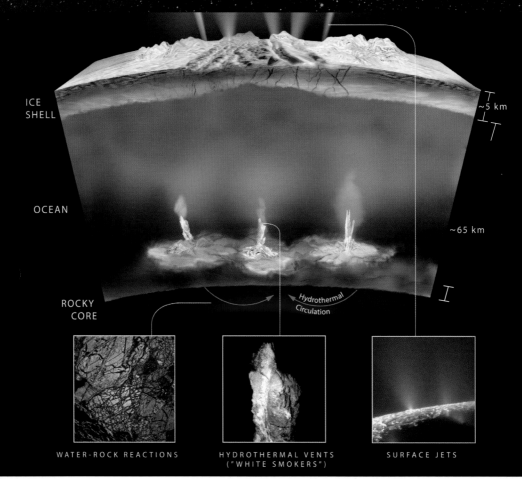

ICE SHELL

OCEAN

ROCKY CORE

~5 km

~65 km

Hydrothermal Circulation

WATER-ROCK REACTIONS

HYDROTHERMAL VENTS ("WHITE SMOKERS")

SURFACE JETS

Deep-Sea Volcanoes Stand in for Space!

In August 2018, NASA's project SUBSEA lowered two robots into a deep-sea volcano off the coast of Hawaii. NASA is using these underwater eruption zones to **mimic** the type of environments robots might find on Saturn's moon Enceladus.

Rollin' Robot to Visit Space

In 2008, German Space Agency DLR unveiled Rollin' Justin. This bot uses AI technology. DLR plans to send it on future Mars missions. Rollin' Justin can clean, catch flying objects, identify materials, and handle tools. The bot may one day act as space sidekick to humans living on Mars!

Lightning-Fast Space Probes

Breakthrough Starshot is a private research and engineering program. It has plans to build tiny space probes to travel to other galaxies in record time. These probes would be **propelled** by light and travel up to 100 million miles (161 million km) per hour!

Glossary

alternating: taking turns or going every other one

analyze: to examine something carefully in order to understand it

cicada: a family of insects with large, transparent wings

efficient: working very well and wasting little time or energy

evidence: information and facts that help prove something true or false

extreme: existing in a high degree

hydrothermal: of or relating to hot water

mimic: to imitate

orbit: to travel in a circular path around something, especially a planet or the sun

permanently: in a lasting way

probes: tools or devices used to explore or examine something

propelled: pushed forward or carried by

satellite: a spacecraft that is sent into orbit around Earth or another body

spacewalks: periods of space activity spent outside spacecraft by astronauts

stranded: left or stuck without the means to move or go somewhere

submarines: a ship that can travel above and below water

technology: the use of science and engineering to do technical things

unique: unlike anything else

wrench: a tool used for tightening and loosening bolts and nuts

Further Information

BOOKS

Fretland VanVoorst, Jenny. *Rovers.*
Minneapolis: Pogo, 2017.
Read more about the many rovers
that have been launched into space.

Furstinger, Nancy. *Robots in Space.*
Minneapolis: Lerner Publications,
2015.
Learn how space robots work and
about the cosmic places they explore!

Nagelhout, Ryan. *Space Robots.*
New York: PowerKids Press, 2016.
Discover space robot history and
find information about the newest
bots in development.

WEBSITES

Idaho Public Television—Robotics:
Facts
http://idahoptv.org/sciencetrek
/topics/robots/facts.cfm
Read about different types of robots,
artificial intelligence, and more.

NASA Space Place—The Mars Rovers
https://spaceplace.nasa.gov/mars
-rovers/en/
Find fast facts about and fun
illustrations of the rover robots
that have traveled to Mars.

Our Universe for Kids—Robot
Explorers
https://www.ouruniverseforkids
.com/robot-explorers/
Photos, facts, and a Question &
Answer section make up this space
robot webpage!

Index